THE
KID'S
GUIDE TO
BOSTON

1st edition

Eileen Ogintz

gpp®
travel

Guilford, Connecticut

Thank you to my daughter Regina, a teacher, who helps me to know just how to engage kids. Thank you to Andrea Timpano and Alexandra Koktsidis for your research help in Boston and to all of the kids who lent their insight about Boston.

Editor: Amy Lyons
Project Editor: Lauren Brancato
Layout: Maggie Peterson
Text Design: Sheryl Kober
Illustrations licensed by Shutterstock.com

ISBN 978-0-7627-9698-4

Printed in China

Contents

1

Welcome to
Beantown!

Ready for some time travel?

Boston is the kind of city where you can wander back nearly 400 years just by taking a walk—or zoom to the very front end of the 21st century the minute you step into the city's cool museums with the latest technology.

Look around! There are skyscrapers right next to very old small buildings next to hip restaurants and shops, some sitting on brick streets.

{ **What's Cool?** Taking a **Boston Duck Tour** on a vehicle that travels on roads— and in the water (617-267-3825; bostonducktours.com). It's a good idea to book reservations. Tours depart from the Prudential Center, the Museum of Science, and shorter tours from the New England Aquarium.

There's another thing about Boston you should know right from the start: Locals are passionate about their city—their sports teams, their politics, and their people. That love came out loud and clear after the Red Sox won the World Series for the first time in 86 years back in 2004, and more recently, after the horrible bombing at the 2013 Boston Marathon when Bostonians showed all of us their strength and their commitment to their city and one another.

Bostonians want visitors to love their city too.

A LOCAL KID SAYS:
"My favorite things to do in Boston are going on the Duck boats, walking and shopping on Newbury Street, and going to the parks."
—Arianna, 13, Walpole, MA

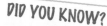

DID YOU KNOW?

Boston is known as Beantown because, in the 18th century, there was a lot of molasses in Boston as a result of its trade with the West Indies. Molasses was made from Caribbean sugarcane, and beans baked in molasses became a favorite local dish.

So make sure you take the time to see some of Boston's **famous neighborhoods** as well as its famous historic sites. A lot of the neighborhoods look different than where you live, and that makes exploring more fun. Families with kids live here in the city as well as in the suburbs. And you'll find people of all sorts in this metropolitan city. Here are some great neighborhoods to visit:

- **BEACON HILL** is famous for its gas-lit streets, brick sidewalks, and beautiful old houses. You'll also find the Massachusetts State House here as well as the famous Boston Common and Public Garden. The Boston Symphony Orchestra has a home here in Symphony Hall.

A LOCAL KID SAYS:
"I like the Swan Boats because you can see all the ducks and the swans in the water."
—Keighan, 9, Revere, MA

■ **BACK BAY** is the place to check out fancy stores on Newbury Street and Copley Place and get a bird's-eye view of the city from the top of the Prudential Center. Back Bay is also where you'll find Boston's famous art museums and Fenway Park where the Red Sox play.

■ **THE WATERFRONT** is where you'll go to stroll along Boston's HarborWalk or visit the New England Aquarium or the Boston Tea Party Museum. The Boston Children's Museum is nearby across the Congress Street bridge.

A LOCAL KID SAYS:
"I like to walk through different areas in Boston and just kinda explore."
—Josh, 12, Sharon, MA

What's Cool? Playing at the Rose Fitzgerald Kennedy Greenway Conservancy and taking a spin on the uniquely Boston carousel—all in sight of Boston's famous harbor (617-292-0020; 185 Kneeland St., Boston, MA 02111; rosekennedygreenway.org).

- **THE NORTH END** is the city's oldest neighborhood—this is where Paul Revere's famous ride started—and one of its most tight-knit with Italian families' restaurants and lots of festivals during the year.

- **THE SOUTH END'S** brick homes have been renovated and house a mix of ethnic groups today.

- **CHARLESTOWN** is where Boston actually started—before the colonists moved their settlement across the river. You'll go to Charlestown to see the famous monument for the Battle of Bunker Hill during the Revolutionary War and the USS *Constitution*, the country's oldest battleship.

DID YOU KNOW?

The creators of that lovable monkey Curious George—Margret and H. A. Rey—lived in Cambridge. Margret Rey was a big supporter of programs for kids at the Boston Public Library. That's why the kids' room at the Central Library in Copley Square (bpl.org/kids) is named for them. Stop in and check out all this amazing library has for kids!

- **ROXBURY** is famous as home to Boston's large African-American community.

- **CHINATOWN** may seem small, but it is the third largest Chinese community in the country, right after those in San Francisco and New York. You can try plenty of good Chinese food here.

- **CAMBRIDGE** is across the Charles River. It is well known as the home of the top colleges Harvard University and MIT.

The hardest decision is where to explore first. Where would you like to visit?

DID YOU KNOW?

On a clear day, you can see up to 100 miles away from the **Prudential Center Skywalk Observatory** (800 Boylston St.; 617-859-0658; topofthehub.com).

A VISITING KID SAYS:
"My favorite things to do in Boston: historical sightseeing, going to Quincy Market, visiting restaurants in the North End, and shopping on Newbury Street!"
—Oona, 14, Portland, ME

7

Riding the T

That's what everyone calls Boston's public transportation system. Have you ever ridden on a trolley? Boston has subways, buses, trolley cars, and even boats that go just about everywhere in the greater Boston area. It's really easy to get around Boston without a car, and kids 11 and younger ride free. You can use the Massachusetts Bay Transportation Authority's trip planner (mbta.com/rider_tools/trip_planner) to figure out which line to take. Different lines are designated by different colors—blue, green, orange, red, and silver. You can also download an app from boston.hopstop.com that will help you navigate. Maybe you can lead the way for your family!

A VISITING KID SAYS:
"Riding the T was better than driving. It was fast!"
—Erica, 13, Newfoundland, Canada

DID YOU KNOW?

The electronic tickets you get to ride the public transit system in Boston are called **CharlieCards.** They are named after a popular old song about a guy called Charlie who didn't have enough money to get off the trolley after the fare increased. The song goes: "Well, did he ever return? No, he never returned, and his fate is still unlearned. He may ride forever 'neath the streets of Boston, he's the man that never returned."

Boston Firsts

Boston is not only one of the oldest cities in the country, but it's also credited with lots of firsts:

- America's first public school (Boston Latin School)
- America's first public library
- America's first public park (Boston Common)
- America's first botanical garden (Public Garden)
- America's first lighthouse, built in Boston Harbor
- America's first meeting house built by free African Americans

A VISITING KID SAYS:
"Boston is really fun, and you learn a lot of history."
—Laci, 14, Lexington, NC

Boston Really Knows How to Party!

That's why a lot of families time their visits to join the fun:

April—Patriots' Day commemorates the anniversary of the Battles of Lexington and Concord on April 19, 1775. Traditionally, it is celebrated the third Monday in April. The Boston Marathon is run on Patriots' Day, and the Boston Red Sox are always scheduled to play at home.

July—On the **Fourth of July** (july4th.org), thousands gather on the DCR Esplanade for a Boston Pops concert and fireworks and come to Boston Harborfest (bostonharborfest.com) with more than 200 activities over the holiday week.

October—Head of the Charles Regatta (hocr.org), the world's largest two-day rowing event, brings thousands of athletes from around the world and hundreds of thousands of spectators to Boston.

December—On **First Night** (firstnightboston.org), Boston celebrates New Year's Eve with kid-friendly activities.

Staying Safe on Vacation

Write down the name and phone number of the hotel where you are staying. Also, write down your parents' phone numbers—or put them in your phone. And carry this record with you wherever you go sightseeing.

- Never approach a vehicle unless you know the owner and are accompanied by an adult.

- Practice "what-if" situations with your parents. What should you do if you get lost in a museum? On a city street? Who should you ask for help?

- Wherever you are, decide on a central, easy-to-locate spot to meet in case you get separated.

- Only ask uniformed people for help if you get lost—police officers, firefighters, store security guards or store clerks, or museum officials wearing official badges or identification badges.

DID YOU KNOW?

Boston's Big Dig highway project was one of the largest and most expensive anywhere in the country. It was finished in 2002 with a new tunnel that moved 200,000 cars a day from the surface roads to underground. The land on top became the Rose Fitzgerald Kennedy Greenway, a 15-acre park.

TELL THE ADULTS:

You don't have to bust the budget to see Boston:

- Your **CharlieCard** electronic MBTA public transit tickets (mbta.com/fares_and_passes/charlie) provide all kinds of discounts.

- The Greater Boston Convention and Visitors Bureau offers a special "Kids Love Boston" family-friendly valuePASS that can get you discounts on everything from food to souvenirs to museums and attractions—over 65 offers. Search for "family-friendly valuePASS" at bostonusa.com to download one for your trip.

- You can also get discounts on major attractions by purchasing a **Boston CityPASS** (citypass.com).

- Visit Boston during restaurant week in March or August and you can try new dishes at restaurants across the city at really reasonable prices with special discounted menus. Lunch is a particularly good deal (bostonusa.com/visit/dineoutboston)!

- Just make sure to leave time to explore Boston's neighborhoods and parks—they are very different from one another. That's where you'll meet local families!

BOSTON "FIRSTS" SCRAMBLE

Since Boston is one of the oldest cities in the country, it's a place where lots of "firsts" happened. Unscramble some of its famous firsts below!

LCOHSO

_____

ULCIPB RRBILAY

_____   _____

PCULIB RAPK

_____   _____

TCAABILON ANDEGR

_____   _____

HSUEGLOITH

_____

GEEMITN EOUSH

_____   _____

See page 153 for the answer key.

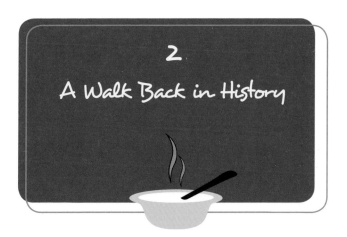

2.

A Walk Back in History

Ready for a walk? It's not just any walk—it's one of the most famous walks in the country.

Welcome to the **Freedom Trail.** This 2.5-mile-long route over brick-lined streets will take you back to a time when Boston was still a colony and people were arguing about what to do about the increasingly difficult demands from the king of England. They didn't think it was fair that the king wanted them to pay taxes when they didn't have any representatives in the English Parliament. But

A VISITING KID SAYS:
"I take pictures of just about everything."
—Christopher, 10, Palm Beach Gardens, FL

DID YOU KNOW?
Three million people—a lot of them parents and kids—walk the Freedom Trail every year.

many people still felt loyal to the king. For many colonists, it was a hard decision. Should they fight for independence? What do you think you would have wanted to do?

Check out some of the historic sites—there are 16—along the way and decide. You'll probably start at the **Boston Common.** It's hard to imagine now, but the Common was sometimes packed with British soldiers. More than 1,000 camped here when the British occupied Boston in 1775.

Wow! The **golden dome** on the Massachusetts State House is impressive. This is one of the oldest buildings on **Beacon Hill.** Paul Revere covered the wood dome with copper long before it was covered with gold. This is where state representatives and the governor run the state government, just like in any capitol.

DID YOU KNOW?

The gold was added to the copper-covered dome of the Massachusetts State House to prevent leaks. It's shiny! There's a wooden pinecone at the very top. That's because logging was very important in Boston during the 18th century.

The steeple of **Park Street Church** is a Boston landmark because it is so tall. This church has always had a big commitment to human rights. Some of the first protests against slavery were made here.

Stop at the **Granary Burying Ground** and see where some of Boston's most famous citizens are buried, including Paul Revere, John Hancock, and Samuel Adams. The victims of the Boston Massacre are buried here too, including a teenaged boy. They died in 1770 when British soldiers opened fire on a crowd that was heckling them. There are a lot more people buried here than there are tombstones.

DID YOU KNOW?

The Boston Tea Party wasn't a tea party at all. It was Patriots dressed as Mohawk Indians who threw 340 crates of tea into the harbor rather than pay the British a tax on the tea. You'll pass the Old South Meeting House on the Freedom Trail where the colonists debated what to do with the tea on December 16, 1773.

A VISITING KID SAYS:
"History isn't boring just because the people are dead. It's about people's lives."
—Ava, 11, Rochester, NY

King's Chapel first was a tiny church used by the British. When the building got too small, the stone structure you see was built around the original wooden church. The builders then threw the wood out the windows piece by piece. Some of Boston's first families are buried here.

How would you like to go to a school that's the oldest public school in the country? Kids still do—at **Boston Latin School**—but just not where the original school was located. You can see Ben Franklin's statue at the site of the school during the Revolutionary War. As smart as he was, he dropped out!

DID YOU KNOW?

Benjamin Franklin grew up in Boston and attended school here with three other signers of the Declaration of Independence—Samuel Adams, John Hancock, and Robert Treat Paine. Look for a statue of Ben Franklin on the Freedom Trail; it stands where the Latin School was located then.

A VISITING KID SAYS:
"Kids should definitely do the Boston Tea Party Museum. You can learn a lot, and it is fun. It was my favorite thing in Boston."
—Alexis, 13, Sugarloaf, PA

You'll pass the **Old South Meeting House** and the **Old State House** where Boston's leading Patriots met and debated British rule before the American Revolution.

All that walking will probably make you hungry.

Good thing your next stop is **Faneuil Hall,** famous for its food court!

Ready for some chowder?

Faneuil Hall

Locals pronounce this "Fan-yoo-ul Hall." It was built in 1742 by a wealthy merchant named Peter Faneuil, who hoped it would be a gathering place and a public market. After the original structure burned down, it was rebuilt. It was in the new hall that many arguments and debates took place about what the colonists should do in the face of increasing pressure from Great Britain before the American Revolution. Then, during the Civil War, abolitionists spoke out against slavery here (1 Faneuil Hall Sq.; 617-523-1300; faneuilhallmarketplace .com). Today citizens' groups still meet here.

Faneuil Hall Marketplace, spread over three long buildings, has become tourism central—a stop on the Freedom Trail and home to more than 75 local shops, restaurants, and stalls. There's North Market, Quincy Market, and South Market. The success of turning this historic building into a popular market and tourist destination led the way for other cities to do the same thing.

DID YOU KNOW?

The grasshopper weather vane of Faneuil Hall is a well-known symbol of Boston. During the Revolutionary War, people would ask suspected spies the identity of the object on top of Faneuil Hall. If they knew the answer, they were freed. If not, they were thought to be British spies.

Black Heritage Trail

While a lot of African Americans were enslaved in the South, Boston was home to a big community of free blacks in the 19th century who led the city and the country in the fight against slavery. They built their own schools, meeting houses, and churches, and they ran businesses. They were leaders in the Abolition movement against slavery, in helping escaped slaves on the Underground Railroad and in the fight for equal rights and education.

Take a walk back in history along the Black Heritage Trail on the north side of Beacon Hill. During the summer, take a tour with National Park rangers (nps.gov/boaf) and become a junior ranger here. You don't want to miss:

A LOCAL KID SAYS:
"Try to learn as much about Boston as you can."
—Nelson, 9, Watertown, MA

- The **Boston National Historical Park Visitor Center,** which is housed in two locations along the Freedom Trail. One is on the first floor of Faneuil Hall. The other is the Charlestown Navy Yard Visitor Center, which is in Building 5 next to the USS *Constitution* in Charlestown, right inside Gate 1 of the Navy Yard.

- The **Abiel Smith School** (the first public school for African-American children) and the **African Meeting House** (the first African Baptist Church of Boston), both located at the **Museum of African American History** in Beacon Hill (46 Joy St.; 617-720-2991; afroam museum.org).

- The **John J Smith House** (86 Pinckney St.) was a place where abolitionists and escaped slaves met.

- The **Lewis and Harriet Hayden House** (66 Phillips St.) was a stop on the Underground Railroad that helped escaping slaves reach freedom.

Paul Revere's Real Ride

The idea was to warn Patriot leaders that the British were marching and to spread the word to everyone else along the way.

It was April 18, 1775, when Boston silversmith Paul Revere, William Dawes Jr., and other Patriots left Boston on their daring mission. While we think it was just Revere, actually there were many riders—so that if one was caught, others would succeed in their mission.

And contrary to Boston poet's Henry Wadsworth Longfellow's famous poem (*"Listen, my children, and you shall hear / Of the midnight ride of Paul Revere"*), on Paul Revere's ride he didn't yell "The British are coming!" He made it to Lexington to warn some of the Patriots but was stopped by the British before he got to Concord and eventually was released without his horse.

Longfellow's poem, written nearly 100 years later and despite the things it got wrong, was credited with turning Paul Revere into a national hero and legend long after his death. Today the famous ride is reenacted every year on Patriots' Day in April.

DID YOU KNOW?

Paul Revere's house is Boston's oldest, dating back to the 1600s. He brought up 16 kids in this house in the North End. You'll find it on the Freedom Trail.

Lexington & Concord

The Battles of Lexington and Concord were the first of the American Revolutionary War—on April 19, 1775.

Today Lexington and Concord are Boston suburbs. Then, they were farms. The fighting started because the British set out to capture military supplies that they thought were stored in Concord. But the Patriots had already moved their supplies. They had gotten word about the British plans, so they were ready.

The first shots were fired at Lexington. Even though the Patriots were far outnumbered by the British, the Patriots forced them to withdraw back to Boston. Ralph Waldo Emerson, in his "Concord Hymn," described the first shot fired by the Patriots at North Bridge as the "shot heard 'round the world."

Today, you can visit the **Lexington Battle Green** (lexingtonhistory.org), **Minute Man National Historic Park** (nps.gov/mima), and **Concord's North Bridge**. You might be able to join a ranger program or see historic reenactors in action. You might even be able to take part!

Explore **Battle Road Trail**—the 5-mile trail that connects the historic sites where the battle was fought. See where Paul Revere was stopped by the British; stop at the Hartwell Tavern to learn how families lived at the time of the American Revolution. Travelers back and forth to Boston stopped here to share the latest news—remember there was no Internet or social media then!

TELL THE ADULTS:

Free is good!

- Thirteen of the 16 attractions along the Freedom Trail (thefreedomtrail.org) are free. You can also join a free National Park Service Tour of the Trail (nps.gov/bost).

- The USS *Constitution* conducts free tours April-September (Charlestown Navy Yard Building 22; 617-426-1812; ussconstitutionmuseum.org).

- Tour the Black Heritage Trail (nps.gov/boaf), the Irish Heritage Trail (irishheritagetrail.com), or the Boston Women's Heritage Trail (bwht.org).

- Take a free tour of Symphony Hall (301 Massachusetts Ave.; 617-638-9390; bso.org).

A VISITING KID SAYS:
"Make sure to wear comfortable shoes. You're going to do a lot of walking in Boston!"
—Laci, 11, Lexington, NC

DID YOU KNOW?

The paving stones of the New England Holocaust Memorial are inscribed with quotes from Holocaust survivors. You'll find the huge glass and steel memorial right beside the Freedom Trail.

- Take a free tour of the Boston Public Library (700 Boylston St.; 617-536-5400; bpl.org). It's an amazing historic building!

- The Isabella Stewart Gardner Museum is always free for those under 18—and anyone named Isabella (280 The Fenway; 617-566-1401; gardner museum.org).

- The Museum of Fine Arts (465 Huntington Ave.; 617-267-9300; mfa.org) is free for kids 7–17 during nonschool hours (weekdays after 3 p.m., weekends, and Boston public school holidays).

- The Institute of Contemporary Art (100 Northern Ave.; 617-478-3100; ica boston.org) is free to kids under 17 years old all the time and free for all every Thursday evening.

- Take a walk along the HarborWalk (bostonharborwalk.com). You can download a free audio tour to your MP3 player!

- Join the locals at the Boston Common (cityofboston.gov/freedomtrail/boston common.asp) and the Public Garden (cityofboston .gov/parks/emerald/public_garden.asp).

- Explore the Road to Revolution in Minute Man National Historic Park outside of Boston in Lexington and Concord (nps.gov/mima).

- Enjoy some music at Jordan Hall, part of the New England Conservatory (30 Gainsborough St.; 617-585-1260; necmusic.edu). Almost all of the concerts are free and do not require tickets, unless other-wise noted on their calendar.

- Catch some outdoor entertainment. Summer con-certs and movies are shown at the DCR's Hatch Memorial Shell outdoor stage on the south bank of the Charles River (47 David G Mugar Way; 617-626-4970; hatchshell.com).

{ **What's Cool?** Eating pizza and gelato in the North End.

HISTORIC BOSTON

Fill in the missing letters to spell out the mystery words.
(You will need to use one of the secret letters twice!)

Boston Co__mon
       (7)

Golden __ome
       (5)

B__acon Hill
 (3)

Park Str__et Church
        (4)

Gr__nary Burying G__ound
  (9)   (2)

K__ng's Chapel
 (10)

Boston __atin School
        (11)

__ld South Meeting House
(6)

Old S__ate House
      (8)

__aneuil Hall
(1)

___ ___ ___ ___ ___ ___ ___   ___ ___ ___ ___ ___
(1) (2) (3) (4) (5) (6) (7)   (8) (2) (9) (10) (11)

See page 153 for the answer key.

3
Bunker Hill, Old Ironsides & Charlestown

Got your climbing shoes on?

Then you are ready to scale the 294 steps to the top of the **Bunker Hill Monument.** It commemorates the first major battle of the Revolutionary War.

Close your eyes and imagine 5,000 troops fighting here. It was June 16, 1775, and only lasted 3 hours, but the clash was a key battle in the fight for American Independence. "Don't fire until you see the whites of their eyes!" the Revolutionary troops were told.

A VISITING KID SAYS:
"My favorite thing to do in Boston is climbing to the top of the Bunker Hill Monument."
—Alex, 12, Weston, CT

The battle was actually fought on Breed's Hill (where the monument is), not Bunker Hill about a half mile away. The colonial militia learned the British planned to send troops to take the hills surrounding the city, and they were waiting at the top of Breed's Hill when the redcoats attacked.

The British won—when the colonial forces ran out of ammunition—but they suffered far greater losses. So that battle proved to everyone that the Revolutionary soldiers were worthy opponents, though they weren't nearly as well trained.

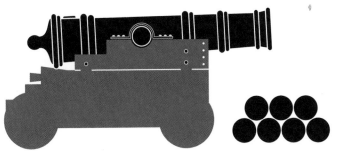

A LOCAL KID SAYS:
"The Freedom Trail is long. Just do part of it. I liked Paul Revere's house because he really lived there."
—Hannah, 11, Natick, MA

If you want to climb to the top of the monument, check to see if you need a free climbing pass. You can do it in the spring and summer, and you can get a pass at the **Bunker Hill Museum** (43 Monument Sq.; 617-242-7275; nps.gov/bost).

The monument and the Bunker Hill Museum are both on the **Freedom Trail,** even though you will have crossed the bridge from Boston into Charlestown.

There's something else on the Freedom Trail you won't want to miss in Charlestown—the **USS *Constitution,*** which is the oldest warship afloat. There's a **USS *Constitution* Museum** (24 5th St., Navy Yard Building 22; 617-426-1812; ussconstitution museum.org) where you can see what it would have been like to be a sailor in the early 1800s. Do you think you could have eaten a biscuit that was as hard as wood?

DID YOU KNOW?

More than 100 African-American and Native American soldiers took part in the Battle of Bunker Hill.

The Freedom Trail continues across the Charlestown Bridge to Charlestown!

A VISITING KID SAYS:
"The Freedom Trail isn't what kids think—a trail in the woods. It's just red bricks on the street in Boston. It is really long but it's interesting."
—Ava, 11, Rochester, NY

Ready to scrub the decks? Boys as young as eight joined the *Constitution's* crew during the War of 1812. Crawl into a hammock and see if you would have liked to sleep there rather than in a bed.

Think you could fire a cannon? Check out the online game and see. In the game, you can try to furl the sail and even see if you're strong enough to haul a goat on board.

What's Cool? The games you can print out or play online from the USS *Constitution* Museum (asailorslifeforme.org/hands_on_activities.php) or the games about the historic sites you're visiting in Boston available from the National Park Service Web Rangers (nps.gov/webrangers).

Now you're probably ready to see the ship. You can take a tour of the USS *Constitution,* which was built in Boston.

While you're at the Charlestown Navy Yard, check out the **USS *Cassin Young,*** a World War II destroyer that is typical of the kind of ships that were built here during that era. Fifty thousand people worked here then!

Whatever the century, it takes lots of hands with many different skills to build and then serve on these US Navy ships.

Would you rather build a ship—or help sail it?

A VISITING KID SAYS:
"The USS *Constitution* was so huge! And it's really old."
—Victor, 12, Rochester, NY

36

Two War Heroes

What was a young doctor doing at the Battle of Bunker Hill? He was an outspoken and committed Patriot. When news reached **Dr. Joseph Warren** of the fighting at Lexington and Concord, he left his patients in the care of an assistant and rode toward the battle. He was elected second general in command of the Massachusetts forces.

When Warren learned the British forces had landed at Charlestown, he didn't take command but joined the fighting men at Breed's Hill where he was killed, becoming an instant hero and a symbol of the sacrifices the young nation was making for freedom.

A little more than a century and a half later, another young officer showed his bravery at Pearl Harbor. **Cassin Young** was awarded the Medal of Honor for his actions at Pearl Harbor, picking up survivors and getting the horrible fires under control. He was killed less than a year later, and the USS *Cassin Young* was commissioned in 1943 in his honor.

DID YOU KNOW?

"Powder monkeys" were young boys who worked aboard warships like the USS *Constitution* during the War of 1812 and carried gunpowder to the cannons on the ship.

The Forgotten War

The British and the Americans were at it again!

The War of 1812 was about issues that had been simmering for a long time, maybe since the American Revolution. The Americans said the British were interfering with trade and illegally seizing American sailors off their ships. But the war really didn't accomplish much, and many call it "the forgotten war"—in between the American Revolution and the Civil War.

After three years of fighting and thousands of casualties, Great Britain agreed to a treaty that really didn't resolve any of the issues that had prompted the US to declare war in the first place.

But there was one lasting positive result for the US. Francis Scott Key was inspired to write the poem that would become the words to the "Star-Spangled Banner" after seeing a giant American flag still flying after the epic battle for control of Fort McHenry in Baltimore.

DID YOU KNOW?

George Washington named the USS *Constitution* after the Constitution of the US. Her nickname is "Old Ironsides" because during the War of 1812, cannonballs fired at her just bounced right off, as if she were made of iron. She's the oldest naval vessel afloat in the world. She's taken out into Boston Harbor every Fourth of July.

It Pays to be Green

Got a reusable water bottle?

It will become a souvenir when you slap stickers on it from all of the places you've visited in Boston. And you'll be helping the planet when you carry it on your walk of the Freedom Trail instead of using disposable plastic water bottles.

You'll be helping the planet too when you take public transportation or walk (Boston is one of the most walkable cities in the country!) rather than drive from place to place.

Boston is serious about being green—from its electric car charging stations to the Hubway bike sharing system (the hubway.com), which allows people to rent bikes around the city in efforts to decrease carbon dioxide emissions.

Here are some other simple things you can do to help the environment while you are in Boston:

Turn off the lights where you are staying when you leave

Recycle

Reuse towels

Take shorter showers

A VISITING KID SAYS:
"My favorite museum is the Old State House Museum because it has really cool things about the 1700s."
—Brian, 10, Weston, CT

SECRET WORD PUZZLE

Using the key, write the letters under the symbols to figure out the secret phrase. Clue: The nickname given to the USS *Constitution* because "cannonballs fired at her just bounced right off."

For example:  = b i r d

See page 154 for the answer key.

NOW TRY AND MAKE YOUR OWN SECRET
MESSAGES IN THE SPACE BELOW.

DID YOU KNOW?

There have been only two father and son pairs who both
served as president of the US. The first two were from
Massachusetts—John Adams (the 2nd president) and
John Quincy Adams (the 6th president). The second two
were George Herbert Walker Bush (the 41st president)
and George Walker Bush (the 43rd president).

TELL THE ADULTS:

Touring historical sites can be exhausting and boring if you're not in the right frame of mind. But you can up the fun quotient very easily:

- Read a kid's book about the American Revolution, some of the Boston Patriots, or the USS *Constitution* before you visit.

- Bring a Frisbee or ball to play with on the Boston Common.

- The kids can become junior rangers when at a National Historical Park.

- When taking guided tours, opt for special family tours when possible. Boston By Foot offers special Boston By Little Feet tours (bostonbyfoot.org), the only walking tour of the Freedom Trail specifically geared to kids.

- There is an app for touring Boston's Freedom Trail (tourbostonsfreedomtrail.com) and one called Boston With Kids from Family iTrips, available from iTunes.

- Use the opportunity to talk about what life would have been like for your family had they lived in Revolutionary War times.

4

The Aquarium,
the Harbor
& the Zoo

Ready to get your hands wet?

At the **New England Aquarium** (1 Central Wharf; 617-973-5200; neaq.org), you've got your choice of touch tanks. Pet a horseshoe crab or get up close and personal with a sea urchin at the **Edge of the Sea Touch Tank.**

Are you brave enough to reach out and touch a shark? They won't hurt you! Step right up to the **Shark & Ray Touch Tank**—the biggest on the East Coast.

It's easy to see why so many kids love the New England Aquarium. There is so much to see and do. And you can travel around the world without leaving the building.

A LOCAL KID SAYS:

"The penguins are so exciting to watch when they dive for food. I'd get a stuffed penguin or a seal as a souvenir because they are *sooo* cute."

—Emma, 10, Newton, MA

Join an expedition to the Amazon Rainforest where you'll see piranhas, electric eels, and poison dart frogs. It's hard to believe those tiny bright blue frogs can be so deadly! Look at the gigantic rain forest trees!

Meet Dory from *Finding Nemo* in the Pacific Reef Community. You'll love all the bright tropical fish. There are 70 different kinds. How many can you name? Look for the sharks hiding underneath the coral.

Maybe you'll want to see one of the **IMAX** nature movies on the largest screen in New England.

{ **What's Cool?** Touching a shark and a ray at the New England Aquarium's big touch tank. Their skin is covered in something called "dermal denticles," which are tiny teeth that help protect them against predators. It feels like sandpaper!

You'll want to spend a lot of time at the **Giant Ocean Tank**. There are thousands of animals here, everything from a scary lionfish—they swallow their food whole!—to a giant Pacific octopus to sharks (look for the blacknose shark) and the aquarium's star **Myrtle the Turtle**. She's lived here for more than 40 years! There are also Kemp's ridley and loggerhead sea turtles. Which is your favorite?

Go outside to see the two families of harbor seals waiting right outside the aquarium's front doors. The Northern fur seals and the California sea lions live in an open-air exhibit too. Watch those California sea lions move! They

DID YOU KNOW?

Every November, the New England Aquarium rescues anywhere from 25 to 150 young sea turtles from the cold waters and beaches of Cape Cod Bay and brings them to the aquarium. Make sure to say hi to Myrtle the Turtle when you visit.

are faster than any other seal or sea lion, swimming at up to 25 miles per hour. That's about five times faster than an Olympic gold medal swimmer.

In case you are wondering about the difference between sea lions and seals: Sea lions have long front flippers that help them "walk" on land, while seals have short front flippers, so if they want to move on land they have to "scoot" on their bellies. Check out their ears too. Seals don't have any ear flaps, just holes where their ears are (and they close these tight when they dive

A VISITING KID SAYS:
"It's the shape of the tank in the aquarium that makes it different. You can see the fish from different angles!"
—Chiara, 12,
Cambridge, England

under water), while sea lions have ear flaps. Sea lions are more social too, always hanging out with, or even on top of, their buddies on rocks. Seals like to have more space while they're lounging around.

Since you're visiting New England, you've got to spend some time at the Gulf of Maine exhibit. The Gulf of Maine includes Boston Harbor and Stellwagen Bank National Marine Sanctuary where you go on **whale-watching trips,** and it stretches all the way to Canada. Here's where you'll see creatures that live nearby—lobsters and giant sea stars, crabs, halibut, and cod (the Massachusetts state fish!).

Who knew there were so many different creatures in the ocean right outside!

DID YOU KNOW?

The Boston Harbor Islands are just a 20-minute boat ride—but a world away—from downtown Boston (bostonharborislands.org)!

34 Islands to Choose From

Visit a Civil War fort, go fishing, explore tide pools, or camp—all within 20 minutes of Boston.

Welcome to the **Boston Harbor Islands National Recreation Area.** You won't want to miss visiting them if you're in Boston in the summer (nps.gov/boha). You can become a junior ranger here too.

Getting to the islands is part of the fun—a quick ferry ride from Long Wharf North Pier (bostonharborislands.org). Watch the skyline along the way!

There are 12 different islands to explore, and 22 more that form an island wilderness. You won't get bored:

- Join a ranger-led kayak lesson off of Spectacle Island.

- Camp in a yurt on Peddocks Island. They've even got bunk beds. All you need to do is bring a pillow and sleeping bag!

- Visit Fort Warren on Georges Island. It was a training camp for Union troops and a depot for Confederate prisoners during the Civil War.

- Have your parents help you find the times of the high and low tides while you are on the islands. At low tide search for tide pools along the shores—you can find sea stars, crab, barnacles, mussels, and more! You don't want to disturb the creatures who call these tidepools home so be careful what you touch and don't take anything with you.

- Count how many birds you see.

Endangered Species & Habitats

An endangered species is an animal or plant that is in danger of disappearing entirely from our planet.

The New England Aquarium has been working to protect ecosystems and conserve threatened animals and habitats for more than 20 years. Some of the work it has done includes helping to protect the North Atlantic right whale, rescuing sea turtles, and researching how to protect the Hector's dolphin, one of the smallest and rarest dolphins in the world.

One of the biggest threats that ocean animals, especially endangered ones, face today is from plastic trash that is floating around their homes. Many animals accidentally eat it, making themselves really sick, or they get tangled up in it, making it really hard for them to swim and breathe. For more information on trash in the ocean, visit marinedebris.noaa.gov. There are lots of things that you can do to help stop more trash from going into the ocean and hurting or even killing animals. Here are a few ideas:

- If you are bringing snacks on your outings around Boston, buy the snacks in bulk and then put them in reusable containers— this way the little plastic wrappers can't end up in the ocean.

- If you are ordering a drink at a restaurant,

politely tell the waiter "no straw please"— straws are a very common piece of trash found in animals' stomachs and on beaches.

- If you are throwing something away, always make sure it goes into the trash—most of the trash that is in the ocean comes from litter on land.

- If you are visiting a beach with your family, take five minutes to pick up what trash you see (except for things that are sharp or dangerous; have your parents pick these up). A little cleanup can help a lot of animals!

A LOCAL KID SAYS:
"You see the harbor seals outside before you even go into the aquarium, and they come right up to the glass to see you."
—Cori, 10, Wellesley, MA

- And if you see a sick or hurt animal on the beach, make sure to alert a grown-up so that the animal can get help!

Whales!

Got your camera? On a **New England Aquarium Whale Watch** (neaq.org/visit_planning/whale_watch) you are guaranteed to see whales. Boston isn't far—by boat—from Stellwagen Bank National Marine Sanctuary, one of the world's most active marine sanctuaries. Whales come here to the mouth of Massachusetts Bay to feed and have fun with other whales. Naturalists on board will tell you about these amazing creatures, but here are some fun facts to start with:

- Humpbacks are 50 feet long and weigh 37 tons! A really neat thing about humpback whales is their fluke (which is their tail). Every humpback whale in the world has a different design on its fluke, just like how every human in the world has a different set of fingerprints. This is how naturalists know who's who when they spot humpbacks in the water!

- Minkes are some of the most common whales in the world today, with a population over one million!

- Finbacks can be as long as 70 feet and weigh 40 tons. Only blue whales are bigger. Some evidence suggests that they can live to be 100 years old!

- White-sided dolphins are only found in the North Atlantic and usually travel in groups, called pods. They love to eat squid, and are different from the three whales mentioned here because they have teeth, and not baleen. (Whales, dolphins, and porpoises are part of the same family. Those longer than nine feet are considered whales and those shorter, dolphins and porpoises.)

Talking to the Animals

Lions, giraffes, or gorillas?

Whatever animals you like, you can see them at **Zoo New England's** (zoonewengland.org) two locations—the **Franklin Park Zoo** in the Boston neighborhood of Dorchester (1 Franklin Park Rd.; 617-541-5466) and **Stone Zoo** in Stoneham, MA (149 Pond St.; 781-438-5100).

You can visit the zoos year-round.

At the Franklin Park Zoo, kids love to go to the Tropical Forest to see the gorillas. You won't want to miss the giraffe family, and the lions in Kalahari Kingdom, where you can climb into a "crashed" Land Rover or see how animals live together in Africa at Serengeti Crossing.

Younger kids especially like Franklin Farm where you can get up close and personal with farm animals like goats and sheep and see newly hatched chicks.

You'll also like the Aussie Aviary—part of the Outback Trail—where you can feed and hold all kinds of brightly colored birds.

Have you ever seen a bald eagle? You can at the Stone Zoo's Yukon Creek. Black bear and reindeer also live here.

Who do you like best?

TELL THE ADULTS:

The New England Aquarium is one of Boston's top tourist attractions, and it can get crowded.

- To make the most of your time, take a virtual tour in advance at neaq.org.

- Buy your tickets online, including for the IMAX theater and the Whale Watch.

- Check the aquarium calendar for special events and family programs.

- Make sure to catch some of the daily presentations that include penguin feedings, seal trainings, and dives in the Giant Ocean Tank.

- Visit the hands-on Edge of the Sea Touch Tank.

- Take a dip with the harbor seals (if the kids are 13) or the northern fur seals (they must be 9) in a special behind-the-scenes program.

- Continue the fun—and learning—at home with the activities the New England Aquarium suggests like making your own sea otter (neaq.org/education_and_activities/games_and_activities/activities).

CONNECT THE DOTS

Peregrine falcons, considered the fastest animal in the world (they have been clocked at over 200 miles per hour while diving), nest in Boston. They can even be found at the top of the Old State House. Look for them in the Greenway parks, especially in the North End. Connect the dots to draw one!

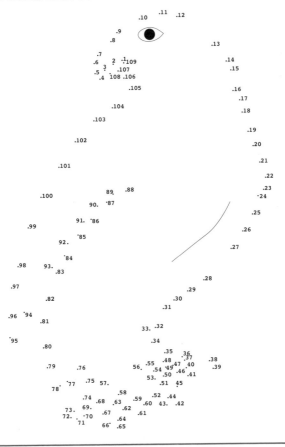

5

The Museum of Science
and
Boston Children's Museum

Name the place in Boston where you can get up close to a giant

triceratops, walk through a butterfly garden, explore the solar system, operate a robot, and learn all about your own body.

Welcome to the **Museum of Science** (1 Science Park; 617-723-2500; mos.org) on land that juts out into the Charles River between downtown and Cambridge.

A LOCAL KID SAYS:
"I like it because it has all different kinds of activities you can do. It's more hands-on."
—Adrien, 14, Oxford, MA

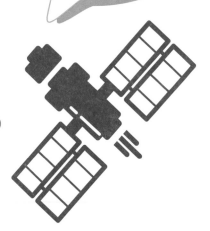

{ **What's Cool?** Joining a drop-in activity like conducting your own experiment or making electricity at the Museum of Science. You can stay overnight at the museum too (mos.org/drop-in-activities)!

There are more than 30 museums in Boston—everything from art museums, to American history museums, to the **Sports Museum of New England,** to a presidential library, to the **Nichols House** on Beacon Hill where you can see what life would have been like if you had lived in the early 1800s (55 Mount Vernon St.; 617-227-6993; nicholshousemuseum.org).

But it's easy to see why kids love the Museum of Science, no matter what their age. This isn't just a science museum. It's also a planetarium, a theater for **IMAX** movies (you'll love the 5-story-tall IMAX Dome screen!), and home to more than 100 animals.

Have you ever seen a cotton-top tamarin? They're South American monkeys that help scientists study animal behaviors. Visit them at the **Live Animal Care Center.**

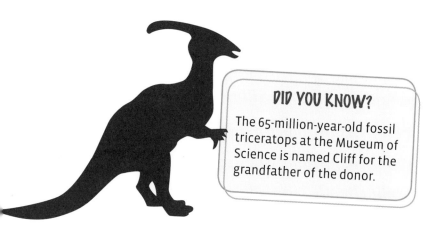

DID YOU KNOW?

The 65-million-year-old fossil triceratops at the Museum of Science is named Cliff for the grandfather of the donor.

The Science Center is so big, with so much to see and do, that it's smart to take a virtual tour before you visit. Where do you want to go first?

There are drop-in activities where you can solve a design challenge by using your engineering smarts. Maybe you'd rather use the same techniques and tools that scientists do in the Hands-On Laboratory. Look for answers in the Investigation Station. Fun!

See a show at the **Charles Hayden Planetarium.** Come on a Friday night and you can join astronomers stargazing after the 7 p.m. show. You can see stars, planets, the moon, and more.

A LOCAL KID SAYS:
"My favorite museum in Boston is the Museum of Science."
—Sydney, 9, Boston

The new Hall of Human Life will teach you about healthy living, while Seasons of Change will teach you about how climate change is affecting the landscape of New England and all the people who live and visit here.

Every day, the museum staff offers **live demonstrations.** Check the schedule to see what's going on when you visit. See indoor lightning bolts or meet some of the furry and scaly creatures who live in the Live Animal Care Center.

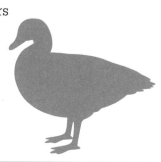

You won't want to miss **Cliff,** the 23-foot-long triceratops. He's big—and one of only four nearly complete triceratops fossils on display anywhere in the world.

Step into one of the museum's simulators take a space walk or search for shipwrecks in a submersible deep under the ocean.

Wow!

A LOCAL KID SAYS:
"I like chasing the butterflies on the screen, making bubbles that are different colors, and playing with the golf balls and dropping them and watching them shoot out."
—Sonia, 6, Walpole, MA

{ What's Cool? Letting off steam in one of Boston's many playgrounds after visiting a museum.

The Power of Play

You may think you're just playing, but you're really learning about the world and yourself.

Kids have been doing that at the Boston Children's Museum for 100 years since it first opened in a house.

Today, it's a huge museum on Boston's waterfront, and museums across the country host exhibits that were created here like Bubbles and Arthur's World based on the book and public TV series featuring the lovable eight-year-old aardvark Arthur Read.

You'll want to challenge yourself on the New Balance Climb. This 3-story climbing structure rises high up through the lobby!

Make art in the museum's Art Studio. Go shopping at a Dominican Store.

Celebrate the history of African Americans in Boston while decorating a float at Boston Black. Everyone loves Bubbles where you can make giant and tiny bubbles. Play checkers on the giant checkerboard in the Common, or try musical chairs—the chairs play the music! Look at the work of local artists in The Gallery. Crawl under the turtle tank to see the resident reptiles in Investigate. Take off your shoes and visit a Japanese House. It was a gift to Boston from the city of Kyoto, Japan.

Check out the huge green roof (ourgreentrail.org)!

Swan Boats, Water Play & More

There's just so much museum-going a kid can take!

That's when it's time to head outside and play, even if you are in the middle of downtown Boston:

- Go to **Charles Bank Playground** right near the Museum of Science. There's even a tunnel for kids to explore.

- Head to the Public Garden adjacent to the Boston Common in summer and ride the famous **Swan Boats** (4 Charles St.; 617-522-1966; swanboats.com). They really look like swans and have been operated by the same family for more than a century!

- See how many flowers you can name at the **Public Garden.**

- Take a **picnic to Boston Common** like locals do.

- Play in the water sprays in Boston playgrounds and parks including the **Frog Pond** in Boston Common (cityof boston.gov/parks/ttd/sprayfeatures.asp).

- Go ice-skating at the Frog Pond in Boston Common in the winter; ride the new carousel in summer (bostonfrog pond.com).

- Hit the playground or watch the sailboats on the river at the **Charles River Esplanade.**

John Fitzgerald Kennedy

John F. Kennedy was the youngest man ever elected US president—he was just 43. He was the fourth US president to come from Massachusetts. The others were John Adams, the 2nd president; his son, John Quincy Adams, the 6th; and Calvin Coolidge, the 30th.

You can learn much more about President Kennedy's legacy, his wife Jacqueline (she was only 31 when she became first lady), and his family at the **John F. Kennedy Presidential Library and Museum** (Columbia Point; 617-514-1600; jfklibrary.org).

The museum and library are set in a 10-acre park landscaped like Cape Cod, where President Kennedy had lived in the summer. In the summer, you can see his sailboat here. You'll see what the Oval Office looked like when he was president—his rocking chair, ship models, and a replica of his desk under which his young son liked to hide.

You can travel back to the 1960s on a kid-friendly tour of the highlights of the museum—you'll even see one of his middle school report cards! Hear the story of how Kennedy's PT-109 patrol boat sank during World War II and his crew's battle for survival. There's even a coconut message that helped save them!

TELL THE ADULTS:

Visiting museums and historic sites can be hard work, especially in a city like Boston where there are so many. Here's how to have more fun—and less anxiety:

- Take a virtual tour before you visit and decide together what you want to see. In big museums like the Museum of Science, it's better to choose what you're most excited about, rather than try to look at everything.

- Make sure that everyone in the family is well rested and has eaten. Have some favorite snacks available in case energy starts to drop.

- Wear comfortable shoes.

- Check out kids' discovery rooms and special drop-in activities for families.

- Divide and conquer! If there are kids at different ages or with different interests, split up and go see different things. When everyone gets back together, share what you've learned!

- Leave when the kids—and you—have had enough and go to a park, playground, or get a snack. The museum will be there the next time you visit!

MUSEUM SCAVENGER HUNT

Look carefully throughout Boston for the following things and check off what you find!

- ☐ Cotton-top tamarin
- ☐ Triceratops
- ☐ Shipwreck
- ☐ Planetarium
- ☐ Butterflies
- ☐ Japanese house
- ☐ Desk from the Oval Office
- ☐ Giant checkerboard

A LOCAL KID SAYS:
"I like the science museum because it has all these cool things to do and the planetarium and IMAX."
—Louise, 13, Milton, MA

6

The Museum Of Fine Arts, Isabella Stewart Gardner Museum, Boston Symphony & More

Where in Boston can you travel across time from ancient Egypt to colonial America to modern times?

The **Museum of Fine Arts** (465 Huntington Ave.; 617-267-9300; mfa.org), of course. This is one of the biggest museums in the entire country—It has more than 460,000 works of arts—so don't expect to see everything at once. Take a virtual tour before you visit. There are so many things to see:

A LOCAL KID SAYS:
"I liked the mummies and the statue of the Egyptian kings."
—Thomas, 8, East Bridgewater, MA

- **Musical instruments.** From around the world, some dating back to ancient times and many that you've never seen or heard of!

- **Jewelry.** Including a tiny bicycle pin with diamond wheels.

- **Textiles.** Boston was once the center of the US textile industry, and you'll see everything here from needlepoint to big tapestries to fashions.

A LOCAL KID SAYS:
"It was really cool seeing glass sculptures."
—Kevin, 13, Newton, MA

DID YOU KNOW?

An orchestra is a group of musicians playing instruments drawn from four different groups—strings, woodwinds, brass, and percussion. Those groups include violins and cellos, flutes, piccolos and clarinets, trumpets and tubas, drums and cymbals, even triangles and bells, among many other options! What would you like to play?

- **Mummies.** There are two rooms of them in the Egyptian collection where you'll also find ancient weapons, coins, and mosaics.

- **Photographs.** The Museum of Fine Arts was one of the first in the country to collect photography.

- **The Art of the Americas.** You can see everything from the Sons of Liberty Bowl that silversmith Paul Revere made to honor the Sons of Liberty, the secret revolutionary organization to which Revere belonged, to amazing model ships.

DID YOU KNOW?

Isabella Stewart Gardner was a friend of leading artists of her time, encouraging music, literature, and dance. She traveled the world to collect her art and built Fenway Court so people could see it. Anyone named Isabella and all kids under 18 get into the museum free!

Don't forget all the paintings, sculptures, and other art from all around the world. Ask your parents to show you the paintings produced by famous artists like John Singer Sargent, Rembrandt, and Claude Monet. This museum has more of Monet's paintings than anywhere else outside of Paris. When you look at these paintings, try to imagine yourself inside the scene!

The Linde Family Wing for Contemporary Art has galleries for multimedia art. Everyone loves *Black River*, a woven tapestry of discarded bottle caps by artist El Anatsui, who is from Ghana. What do you think of it?

A LOCAL KID SAYS:
"I liked seeing the mummies and the exhibit on ancient coins."
—Mary, 11,
East Bridgewater, MA

The best part about this museum is that there are so many programs to help you explore. There are special kids' art classes. Look for the **Family Art Cart** with special fun activities. Pick up **Art Connections Cards** that share fun facts about what you are seeing in the different galleries.

Ask when you arrive where you can check out a **Family Activity Tote** with a sketchbook and colored pencils. Are you ready to create your own masterpiece?

What's Cool? The Family Art Carts at the Museum of Fine Arts.

Music Everywhere!

Vacations are a good time to do something you haven't done—like attend a concert showcasing music you might not hear every day. Check out the interactive music games on the Boston Symphony Orchestra website (bso.org/swfs/games/CatchyTuba).

There are plenty of opportunities to hear different kinds of music in Boston, and it doesn't have to bust the budget:

Go to a free **Boston Pops** concert at the Hatch Memorial Shell in the summer (hatchshell.com).

Visit Trinity Church (trinitychurchboston.org) to hear the **Trinity Choristers.** They often sing on Wednesday at 5:45 p.m. and on Sunday at 9 a.m.

Attend a **Boston Symphony Orchestra** family concert (bso.org).

Try out a concert at the **Isabella Stewart Gardner Museum** (gardnermuseum.org/music) or at the **Institute of Contemporary Art** (icaboston.org/programs/performance).

Find out what's new at a concert that showcases students and faculty at the **Berklee College of Music** (berklee.edu/events/concerts).

Go to a free concert at the **New England Conservatory** (necmusic.edu).

Attend a concert of the **Boston Philharmonic Youth Orchestra** (bostonphil.org).

Art, Gardens & Music

Wow! The inside courtyard at the **Isabella Stewart Gardner Museum** combines bright flowering plants and ancient sculptures. It's a fun place for kids to explore.

Isabella Stewart Gardner would have been an interesting person to meet. She loved art and culture, but she also loved the Red Sox and Harvard football. She traveled the world to collect art and then built her museum to share her collection with the community in what was then a new neighborhood of Boston. You can see a famous portrait of her in the museum.

The museum isn't like most others you've visited. It's modeled on a palazzo you might find in Venice, Italy. Gardner especially loved Venice.

There are a series of rooms that surround the courtyard—the Spanish Cloister, the Early Italian Room, the Dutch Room, and the Yellow and Blue Rooms among them. You'll find everything from famous paintings to tapestries to sculptures to musical instruments and furniture—more than 2,000 objects. This museum has a lot more to offer than paintings on the wall! You can download family guides that will help you understand what you are seeing, or ask for them when you visit.

Make sure you don't touch anything—the art, the walls, or the furniture. Even the lightest fingers can cause damage! All of the objects were placed where you see them today by Gardner herself more than 100 years ago.

The recently built Piano building, named for the architect Renzo Piano, includes a concert hall and space for contemporary art. Do you like the art here better?

Stop in at the Living Room to learn more about the art you've just seen. Volunteers there can answer your questions.

What did you like best?

A VISITING KID SAYS:
"The Isabella Stewart Gardner Museum, near the Boston Latin School, is my favorite museum in Boston. It's a beautiful museum, and definitely worth a visit. It has the best collection I've ever seen in a museum!"
—Oona, 14, Portland, ME

TELL THE ADULTS:

Visiting an art museum can be a real adventure! The museums have tips to make the most of your visit and suggestions for how visiting any art museum can be more fun:

- Kids under 17 are admitted to the Museum of Fine Arts (465 Huntington Ave.; 617-267-9300; mfa .org) free after 3 p.m. on weekdays and all day on weekends. Kids are also free at the Institute of Contemporary Art, so parents shouldn't feel guilty just spending an hour or two.

- Seek out family guides. Download self-guided activity sheets or pick up a copy at the Sharf Visitor Center at the Museum of Fine Arts (mfa .org/programs/kids-and-family-programs/art-connections). You can pick up a free booklet for families at the visitor center at the Institute of Contemporary Art and download family guides at the Isabella Stewart Gardner Museum (gardner museum.org/education/programs_and_resources/ family_resources).

- Look closely at the art and encourage the kids to imagine the sights, sounds, and smells you would experience if you stepped inside. Strike a pose like the sculptures.

- Create a theme. Search for faces, crowns, animals, or particular shapes. How many zigzags do you see? How many paintings have yellow or blue in them?

- Sketch what you see. The Sharf Visitor Center offers a tote bag you can borrow with drawing materials.

- Play "I Spy" in one gallery.

- Pick two similar works of art and compare how they are alike and different.

- Don't feel like you need to see an entire museum in one day. These are big places and worth many visits!

- Keep the art conversation going when you leave. What was everyone's favorite object?

Music, Theater & Art

They're all part of what you'll experience at **the Institute of Contemporary Art** (100 Northern Ave.; 617-478-3100; icaboston.org), starting with the amazing building.

It's on the Boston waterfront, and the huge windows let you get a different view from wherever you are in the museum.

There is contemporary art here in all forms. That includes music, film, video, and performance art. You might see story-tellers, musicians, dancers, or a movie here. You might have the chance to meet some of the artists. Every summer, there are free concerts on the waterfront presenting musicians from Boston's Berklee College of Music.

As soon as you go inside, you'll spot the Sandra and Gerald Fineberg Art Wall where you'll see new original work commissioned each year. It's fun to check out the harbor from the huge glass walls in the elevator.

See what special programs for kids are going on in the Education Center.

Visit the Poss Family Mediatheque to learn more about the artists at the digital media center. You can also offer your own opinion about what you've seen.

Are you ready to say what you think?

{ **What's Cool?** Going to an outdoor concert in Boston in the summer.

DO-IT-YOURSELF CRAFT

Famous sculptor Alexander Calder loved making things
from everyday objects when he was a child. He created an
entire miniature circus out of wire, fabric, and other materials he found, and invited friends over for circus shows.
Look for his wonderful sculpture of a cow made out of wire
in the American Modernism gallery at the Museum of Fine
Arts. What kind of sculpture would you make?

Materials:
clothes hanger, string, poster board
Activity:
Cut the poster board into interesting shapes.

Poke a small hole somewhere on the shape and tie
a piece of string to each shape. Hint: Use different
lengths of string and various shapes for interest.

Tie string to the clothes hanger to create your own mobile.

7
Across the River in Cambridge

Do you like inventing things?

You'd fit right in at **Harvard University** and **MIT**. Facebook was invented at Harvard; e-mail was invented by an MIT graduate and the World Wide Web by an MIT professor.

The students who go to Harvard and MIT are some of the best students in the country. They study every subject you can think of and come from around the world. The two schools are in different parts of Cambridge, and if you visit both, you'll see they have totally different vibes.

Harvard, founded in 1636, was the first college in North America. The idea behind the school was to educate young men for the

A VISITING KID SAYS:
"The campuses are beautiful, and the whole town is amazing and exciting. There is always something to do."
—Dana, 14, Holmdel, NJ

ministry. That's why when you walk through Harvard Yard, you'll see many very old buildings. It's hard to believe now, but women weren't allowed to attend college until almost 250 years later, and even then, they had a separate school—Radcliffe College—where they were taught by Harvard faculty. The two schools really didn't completely merge until 1999. It shows you how much education for women has changed!

A LOCAL KID SAYS:
"I really like the Harvard Museum of Natural History. Each room is like being in a different place, and it is really cool!"
—Caroline, 9, Boston

What's Cool? The robots at the MIT Museum.

A lot of families live in Cambridge, and there are plenty of places to play and ride bikes, especially along the **Charles River.** Kids like to shop in **Harvard Square** because there are so many stores. There are plenty of places to eat too. Listen to the conversations going on around you. How many different languages do you recognize? You'll see street performers and people wearing every kind of outfit.

Walk around Cambridge near Harvard Square, especially on Brattle Street, and you'll see lots of historic buildings and houses—some even dating back to before the American Revolution. Brattle Street was once called "Tory Row" because, in the years leading up to the American

A VISITING KID SAYS:
"Harvard Square was a lot busier than I thought it would be. I really like to visit art museums and look at the paintings, but not modern ones."
—Victor, 12, Rochester, NY

DID YOU KNOW?

There's a 42-foot-long skeleton of a kronosaurus, an underwater dinosaur that lived during the early Cretaceous period, at the Harvard Museum of Natural History. Kronosaurus means "titan lizard."

Revolution, the mansions here were owned by supporters of King George, known as Tories. The mansions were taken over by Patriots when supporters of American independence came into control of Cambridge in 1775. You can visit the **Hooper-Lee-Nichols House** (159 Brattle St.; 617-547-4252; cambridgehistory.org/HLN) and the **Longfellow House–Washington's Headquarters National Historic Site** (105 Brattle St.; 617-876-4491; nps.gov/long).

When you go to MIT—which is short for the Massachusetts Institute of Technology—in another part of Cambridge, it's as if you are in a totally different world. MIT wasn't founded until 1861, and it didn't move to Cambridge along the Charles River until more than 60 years later. The first woman student was admitted within 10 years of MIT's founding. Today, of course, there are many young women who study both at Harvard and MIT and the other colleges and universities in and around Boston.

The emphasis at MIT has always been on science and, more recently, technology and economics. A lot of early research on computer technology was done here—and this field continues to be a focus at the school.

Check out all the **giant sculptures** on the MIT campus. They are cool! *Elmo-MIT* by Dimitri Hadzi was the first outdoor sculpture at MIT. You'll also like *TV Man* by David Bakalar. You'll find both near the Hayden Library.

MIT Museum

Moving sculptures ...
holograms ... robots.

Who says science
is boring? It's not at
the interactive **MIT
Museum** (265 Massachu-
setts Ave.; 617-253-5927; web
.mit.edu/museum).

A VISITING KID SAYS:
"I like all the artificial
intelligence information in the
MIT Museum."
—Ian, 14, New Orleans, LA

Learn all about how robots interact with their environ-
ments or are used in specialized fields such as surgery. They
sometimes seem like humans! MIT has been a leader in artificial intelligence research for more than 50 years.

Throughout the school year, there are hands-on work-
shops and drop-in activities. See what is scheduled when you
are going to be there. On the day after Thanksgiving, adults
and kids link mini chain reactions devices they have made at
home together, forming one huge chain reaction. Think of set-
ting up dominos to fall in neat patterns—just with much more
complicated sets of cascades and lots of interesting people
and creations. Fun!

All of the exhibits blend art and science. Check out the
moving kinetic art in *5000 Moving Parts*.

Did you know you could be a scientist *and* an artist?

College Central

It is no wonder you see students wherever you go. There are more colleges and universities in and around Boston than anywhere in the world—big ones and small ones, on city streets and secluded campuses in Boston, Cambridge, and the other neighboring towns. Walk through a campus and think about where you might want to go to college someday. In Boston you can study just about anything—engineering and music, law and medicine, art and education at these schools:

Berklee College of Music

Boston University (BU)

Boston College (BC)

Brandeis University

Emerson College

A VISITING KID SAYS:
"Get a Harvard sweatshirt as a souvenir."
—Rebecca, 10, Lockport, IL

DID YOU KNOW?

Harvard University is the oldest institution of higher learning in the US. It was named for John Harvard, a young minister who was the school's first financial backer. When he died two years after the school was founded, he left his library and half of his estate to the school. You can see a statue of John Harvard in Harvard Yard.

Harvard University

Massachusetts College of Art (MASSART)

Massachusetts Institute of Technology (MIT)

New England Conservatory (NEC)

Northeastern University

Simmons College

Tufts University

University of Massachusetts Boston (UMB)

Wellesley College

And that's just some of the better known options. Do you think you'd like to go to college in Boston?

Sightseeing Smarts

Sightseeing can be hard work, especially in a city like Boston with so much to see. Here's how to make sure you have lots of fun exploring:

Wear comfortable shoes.

Compromise with your family so that all members get to visit something they are looking forward to seeing.

Bring a map or program one into your smartphone so you know where you are going. There are many free apps that can help too.

Stash some snacks and a reusable water bottle in your backpack. Buy stickers for your water bottle wherever you go!

Alternate museums and historic sites with time in a playground or park. That way you won't get so tired!

When you get really tired, take a break or quit for the day. There will be more to see tomorrow!

DID YOU KNOW?

Harvard's Widener Library is named for Harry Elkins Widener, a 27-year-old book lover who had gone to Harvard and died along with his father on the ship *Titanic* when it sank. His mother donated the money for the library in his memory. Today Widener is one of the largest libraries in the world—the only bigger library in the US is the Library of Congress.

Harvard Museums

What's your favorite flower?

The **Harvard Museum of Natural History** (26 Oxford St.; 617-493-3045; hmnh.harvard.edu) has a collection of 3,000 flowers. Did we mention they are all made out of glass? They look totally real!

Kids also love this museum because of the stuffed lifelike animals that are exhibited as if they were alive. There are sparkling gemstones, fossils, and animal skeletons. The Evolution exhibit has a Tree of Life Touch Table that will help you understand how we all have evolved.

A VISITING KID SAYS:
"The dinosaurs are pretty cool. I like the big one on the wall."
—Hector, 11, Madrid, Spain

There are a lot of interactive exhibits at this museum. Also at Harvard, there's the **Peabody Museum of Archeology and Ethnology** (11 Divinity Ave.; 617-496-1027; peabody.harvard.edu) where you can learn how the Native Americans dealt with the arrival of Europeans in the New World. Check out the Storied Walls that tell you about ancient wall paintings around the world.

TELL THE ADULTS:

Let someone else navigate! Check the Boston official tourism site for special family options at bostonusa .com. Give yourself a break—just for a few hours— and let someone else lead the way. Here are six tours that win kudos from families:

- **Urban AdvenTours** offers bike tours (103 Atlantic Ave.; 617-670-0637; urbanadventours.com). They have kids' bikes and helmets as well as child seats and trailer bikes. If you prefer to ride by your- selves on one of the many bike paths in Boston and Cambridge, they can deliver your rental bike to wherever you are staying. (The wonderful new Hubway bike sharing system doesn't have kids' bikes and you have to bring your own helmet.)

- **Boston Duck Tours** (bostonducktours.com) carry you around the city in a WW II–style amphibious landing vehicle, which means you cruise by all the historic sites and then your Duck will splash into the Charles River for a special view of the Boston and Cambridge skylines. And all along the way, drivers keep the kids engaged with a running com- mentary. They might even let them help steer!

- **Old Town Trolley Tours** (888-910-8687; trolley tours.com/boston) was the city's first hop-on hop-off tour—there are many different companies that you can choose from, especially near Faneuil Hall or the New England Aquarium. You pay one price and can hop off and on at various sites while the conductors tell you what you are seeing. There are historic tours, ghost tours, historic Ball Park Tours, and even a chocolate tour. The conductors pride themselves on their storytelling ability, and you can start the tour at any of their 20 stops. You can save money if you buy your tickets online!

- **Codzilla** (Long Wharf; 617-227-4321; bostonharbor cruises.com/codzilla) is a boat, painted to look like a mean fish, with a unique hull so that it can spin and turn quickly. It's the only high-speed thrill boat in Boston Harbor and offers a high-speed, 40-minute ride. This excursion is meant for summer. Get ready to get wet!

- **Boston Harbor Cruises,** the same company that operates *Codzilla,* offers cruises around Boston Harbor, to Provincetown at the tip of Cape Cod, to Salem, and whale-watching trips through a part-nership with the New England Aquarium (boston harborcruises.com).

- **Boston By Foot** offers many walking tours, includ-ing special ones for the holidays and during Harborfest in July, showcasing the seafaring heri-tage of Boston. There are special Boston By Little Feet tours of the Freedom Trail (8 Faneuil Hall Marketplace; 617-367-2345; bostonbyfoot.org).

What's Cool? The food trucks in Cambridge. Look for tacos, Asian noodles, Chinese stir-fries, lobster rolls, and desserts.

WORD SEARCH: COLLEGE CENTRAL

Circle the names of these colleges and universities.

Berklee
Boston College
Emerson
NE Conservatory
Northeastern

Boston University
Brandeis
MASSART
Tufts

MIT
Wellesley
UMB
Simmons

```
B  O  S  T  O  N  U  N  I  V  E  R  S  I  T  Y
A  O  A  B  V  A  S  U  V  S  E  T  O  W  D  R
B  M  S  M  R  C  O  E  U  E  G  A  A  N  G  O
E  B  R  T  B  S  I  M  M  O  N  S  L  O  T  T
R  R  E  C  O  F  A  E  B  A  H  T  R  R  N  A
T  A  A  N  L  N  E  R  R  T  T  A  T  A  V
U  N  T  Q  L  C  C  S  V  P  Y  S  O  H  B  R
F  D  A  Z  B  O  N  O  M  N  S  E  S  E  T  E
T  E  R  Y  O  C  C  N  L  A  E  G  S  A  P  S
S  I  I  O  R  A  H  L  M  L  T  R  I  S  R  N
Y  S  O  Y  E  L  S  E  L  L  E  W  L  T  I  O
J  U  S  M  S  O  C  D  N  A  L  G  N  E  W  C
E  C  M  I  T  N  R  S  E  W  R  E  E  R  O  E
B  E  R  K  L  E  E  M  O  N  I  C  A  N  Q  N
```

See page 154 for the answer key.

8

Boston Sports

Got your Red Sox cap? If not, a shirt will do.

You probably don't want to go to a Red Sox game in **Fenway Park** without becoming an honorary fan. People in Boston take their sports seriously, and that's especially the case in historic Fenway Park where the Red Sox play. After all, they call Boston **"Red Sox Nation!"**

Fenway is a lot different than modern major league parks. For one thing, it's so old that it's on the National Register of Historic Places. It's still got some of the original seats!

See the **Green Monster?** It's not a creature but rather the giant green wall over left field. People say The Monster lets balls that would have been outs in other ballparks become home

DID YOU KNOW?

The name Red Sox refers to the red socks in the team uniform. The name Fenway Park came from the park's location in the Fenway neighborhood.

The inside of the Green Monster—the wall over left field—at Fenway Park is packed with signatures left by current and former major league baseball players.

runs here. If you take a tour, you may get to go to the top of the Green Monster.

Did you notice that the bleacher seats are green—except for one red one? That's in honor of the **longest home run** ever hit in Fenway Park—502 feet!

No worries if you aren't visiting Boston during baseball season. Bostonians are just as enthusiastic about their other teams. What's your favorite pro sport? Depending on when you visit, you can watch the **Bruins** play hockey, the **Celtics** play basketball, or the **Patriots** play football just outside of Boston.

It's fun to watch **college sports** in Boston too because there are so many different ones—rowing crew on the Charles River, football, swimming, track and field, fencing, lacrosse, soccer, golf, tennis, and hockey among them. . . . Maybe you'll want to play a college sport someday!

But you don't have to wait to play outside in Boston—no matter what the season. There's a lot more to do in Boston than visit historical sites and museums! Whatever the time of year, kids in Boston like to play outside. This is a city where you might have the chance to try something you've never done:

Fish in **Jamaica Pond** (jamaica pond.com) in the Jamaica Plain neighborhood.

Sail or kayak on the **Charles River.**

Explore the tide pools and beaches at **Boston Harbor Islands,** a short ferry ride from the Boston Harbor (bostonharborislands.org).

Meet local kids in one of Boston's many playgrounds, such as **Christopher Columbus Waterfront Park** on Atlantic Avenue.

Go for a hike. The **Blue Hills Trailside Museum** offers some organized nature walks (mass audubon.org).

A LOCAL KID SAYS:
"People in Boston really love their teams. They paint their faces green for the Celtics!"
—Caroline, 9, Boston

In winter, ice-skate on the **Frog Pond** in the Boston Common or the lagoon in the Public Garden. You might find a pickup ice hockey game there!

Cycle on one of Boston's many bike paths.

What's your pick?

{ **What's Cool?** Taking a sailing lesson on the Charles River with Community Boating (community-boating.org). There are also rowing classes (communityrowing.org).

Boston Strong

The Boston Marathon is one of the most important footraces in the world. It's held every Patriots' Day (the third Monday in April), and people come from around the world to run and to cheer the runners. Adults can't just sign up to run the Boston Marathon. They have to qualify with a certain time in another marathon, unless they are running for charity.

In 2013, the whole world watched in horror when two bombs went off near the finish line of the race. Kids who live in Boston and those who like to visit were just as upset as grown-ups.

What happened was terrible, but it is important to remember that Bostonians have a very strong spirit and have refused to let one senseless violent act destroy their city. They came up with a motto of BOSTON STRONG to stay positive. You'll see "Boston Strong" shirts, car decals, bracelets, caps, and more when you visit.

DID YOU KNOW?

The Boston Marathon is the world's oldest continuously run marathon. The first race was on April 19, 1897. Only 15 men ran that day; today more than 25,000 men and women come to run from around the world.

Souvenir Smarts

Do you want a Red Sox cap, a Harvard sweat-shirt, or a plush penguin from the New England Aquarium? The hardest part will be deciding what to buy.

- Shop smart! That means talking to your parents about exactly how much you may spend. Save your pennies and quarters before you visit. Some families save loose change in a jar to use for vacation souvenirs. Got any birthday money you can add?

I ❤ BOSTON

A VISITING KID SAYS:
"The tour of Fenway and the game were so fun. We got jersey shirts."
—Max, 8, Toronto, Canada

- Do you want to use your money for one big souvenir or several smaller ones?

- Resist those impulse buys and think about choosing something you could only get in Boston.

- Start a collection! Buy stickers to put on your reusable water bottle. Collect pins or patches to put on your backpack. What else could you collect?

Hiking Smarts

There are a lot of places around Boston to go for a hike. The area is especially pretty in the fall when the leaves are changing colors! Make sure to hike smart:

- If you get separated from the group, "hug a tree" and stay where you are until your parents return.

- Make sure you have their cell phone numbers and where you are staying written on a card in your pocket, just in case you forget.

- Have a reusable water bottle and healthy snacks in your backpack.

- Use sunscreen, even if it is cloudy.

- Bring rain gear. The weather can change quickly!

- Remember it is about the journey! If someone gets tired or the hike is too difficult, just turn back.

Where to Catch the Action

Whatever season you visit Boston, there will be professional sports going on followed by some of the most enthusiastic fans you'll find anywhere:

The Boston Red Sox play baseball at Fenway Park (4 Yawkey Way; 877-733-7699; boston.redsox.mlb.com).

The New England Patriots play football at Gillette Stadium in Foxborough (1 Patriot Place; 508-543-8200; patriots.com).

The Boston Celtics play basketball at TD Garden (100 Legends Way; 617-624-1050; nba.com/celtics).

The **Boston Bruins play hockey at TD Garden** (100 Legends Way; 617-624-1050; bruins.nhl.com).

The **Head of the Charles Regatta** (mid-October) hosts rowers from around the world competing in races on the Charles River (hocr.org).

> ### DID YOU KNOW?
>
> Both the Boston Celtics basketball team and the Boston Bruins hockey team play their home games at TD Garden.

College Sports in Boston

at Harvard . . . . gocrimson.com

at Boston College . . . . . bceagles.com

at Boston University . . . . goterriers.com

A LOCAL KID SAYS:
"Red Sox games are fun because you can catch a ball or eat cotton candy. When someone scores a home run, the crowd goes wild, and it's so cool to see."
—Arianna, 13, Walpole, MA

DID YOU KNOW?

Fenway Park, where the Boston Red Sox play, is more than 100 years old. It's the oldest ballpark still in use in major league baseball. The Red Sox have played here since 1912; they won the World Series that year too. You can take a tour of the park (boston.redsox.mlb.com).

MATCH THE TEAM WITH THE SPORT

Boston is a sports town. From the Green Monster at Fenway to the ice at the TD Garden, you'll find the faithful in their team colors in support of their sport.

Match the team with the sport

Red Sox	Football
Patriots	Hockey
Celtics	Baseball
Bruins	Basketball

See page 155 for the answer key.

A LOCAL KID SAYS:
"I also like to go to sports games—
Red Sox, Celtics, Bruins—because they are
lots of fun and there are tons of people
cheering on their favorite pro players!"
—Sami, 13, Walpole, MA

9
Boston Souvenirs & Good Eats

Did all that sightseeing make you hungry?

You'll find plenty of food you like in Boston—pizza and hot dogs, burgers and ice cream.

But Boston is a good place to try some new food—like New England **clam chowder** or seafood caught right off the coast of Massachusetts.

Maybe you'd rather have a Chinese noodle dish in Boston's **Chinatown.**

A VISITING KID SAYS:
"I had clam chowder in a bread bowl. I'd never had that before, and it was really good."
—Laci, 14, Lexington, NC

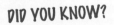

DID YOU KNOW?

Boston's Chinatown is the third largest in the country, after those communities in San Francisco and New York City. Today you will find other Asian restaurants here as well as Chinese—Vietnamese, Korean, Japanese, and Thai among them.

You'll find anything in Boston from fancy restaurants to burger places to the stands in Faneuil Hall Marketplace where you can get everything from the biggest chocolate chip cookies you've ever seen to Indian curry, sushi, barbecue, bagels, paninis, and all varieties of **New England seafood**—fried fish-and-chips, steamed clams and lobsters, and raw oysters that are considered a delicacy. Do you think you'd like to try one? They really taste like the ocean. Boston is one place where every person in the family can get exactly the food they crave without compromising!

A LOCAL KID SAYS:
"Kids should try seafood while in Boston, considering we're right by the ocean."
—Nicole, 14, Waltham, MA

In summer, you can stop at one of Boston's **farmers' markets** and pick up yummy fixings for a picnic in the park. You'll find them all around the city on different days—from Copley Square to the Prudential Center to Cambridge. Ask at your hotel or do a quick online search to find one where you are going to be (massfarmersmarkets.org). Talk to the farmers about what they grow.

A VISITING KID SAYS:
"Try all the samples of food at Faneuil Hall."
—Noah, 14, Princeton, NJ

DID YOU KNOW?

Kids in Boston like to go to "The Pru"—the Prudential Center—for the view from the top and to shop in all the stores (800 Boylston St.; 617-236-3100; prudentialcenter .com). It's a huge mall—great for a rainy day and when you've had enough of museums and historic sites!

A lot of kids like to go to the **North End** for lunch or dinner. Your parents will probably take you here because it is home to two of the Freedom Trail's most visited sites— the Paul Revere House and the Old North Church. This is where Paul Revere's ride started, and many consider it the birthplace of the American Revolution because a lot of the first planning against England was organized at homes and taverns here. This is also where you can get some of the best pizza, pasta, and gelato in the city.

{ What's Cool? Sampling a flavor of gelato you've never had in the North End.

Are you full yet? Then it's time to do some **shopping.** Will it be a Harvard sweatshirt or a Red Sox cap? They're two of the souvenirs visiting kids like to get. Maybe you want to buy a book that is set in Boston—like Robert McCloskey's classic *Make Way for Ducklings,* about the mallard family who decide to live in the Public Garden. It's the **official children's book of Massachusetts.**

You can find everything with Boston on it too. How about a T-shirt with a map of Boston, a tote, a stuffed bear, key chains, or magnets?

DID YOU KNOW?

Newbury Street stretches for 8 blocks—just under a mile. It's Boston's top shopping area—and good for people-watching too.

Maybe you want a pair of socks with tiny lobsters on them? Faneuil Hall Marketplace is **souvenir-central** where you'll find those and likely anything else you want to buy at its small stands as well as the mainstream shops just outside.

Kids also like to shop in **Harvard Square** as well as along **Newbury Street.** You'll find little local boutiques and fancy name-brand stores.

What's your souvenir pick?

DID YOU KNOW?

New Balance is headquartered in Boston. You can visit the New Balance Factory Store at 40 Life St. in Brighton (617-779-7429; newbalance.com) and then try out your new sneakers at the nearby Portsmouth Playground.

Souvenir Stops

EVERYTHING RED SOX: Yawkey Way Store (19 Yawkey Way; 800-336-9299; yawkeywaystore.com)

EVERYTHING NEW ENGLAND: Best of Boston (Faneuil Hall Marketplace and Prudential Center; 617-227-3962)

LOCAL CRAFTS: Original artwork, handmade jewelry, light-up T-shirts, and more at Faneuil Hall's 100+ shops and pushcart vendors (4 S. Market St.; 617-523-1300; faneuil hallmarketplace.com)

> A LOCAL KID SAYS:
> "I get magnets as souvenirs wherever I go and put them on the magnetic wall in my room."
> —Cori, 10, Wellesley, MA

EVERYTHING HARVARD: Almost anything you can think of with the Harvard logo and all kinds of books at Harvard Book Store in Cambridge (1256 Massachusetts Ave.; 617-661-1515; harvard.com)

CURIOUS GEORGE?: Yep! The world's only Curious George Store full of Curious George apparel, toys, games, and puzzles, some of which cannot be purchased anywhere else in the world is located in Cambridge (1 JFK St.; 617-547-4500; thecuriousgeorgestore.com)

How to Eat a Lobster

Your parents have let you order a lobster—even though it is expensive—or share theirs, perhaps at **Summer Shack** (50 Dalton St.; 617-867-9955; summershackrestaurant.com) or one of the many **Legal Sea Foods** restaurants around Boston and Cambridge. Now what? Here's how the Gulf of Maine Research Institute—most of the lobsters we eat come from Maine—says you should go at it:

- Take off the claws and twist off the loose part of the claw.

- Use a nutcracker to crack the claw.

- Push the meat with your finger from the tip of the claw out of the larger open end.

- Twist and separate the tail section and then push the tail meat out. (You may need help or a knife to open the tail section.)

- Dip in butter and enjoy!

- If you are a really adventurous eater, you might want to dig out tiny morsels of meat from the rest of the shell. You'll also encounter the tomalley (it's green and the lobster's digestive system) and roe (it's red and the lobster's unfertilized eggs). Lobster lovers like to eat the roe.

- Ready for another one, or was it too much work?

Good Eats

Vacation is always a good time to try something new to eat, and you can easily do that in Boston. Here are some things you could sample:

- **Pizza at Regina's** original location in the North End (11½ Thacher St.; 617-227-0765; reginapizzeria.com), though now you can get it all around the city. It's considered Boston's best pizza and has been a Boston tradition for more than 80 years!

- **Cannoli, a pastry filled with sweet creamy filling, at Mike's Pastry** in the North End (300 Hanover St.; 617-742-3050; mikespastry .com).

> A LOCAL KID SAYS:
> "Regina's pizza is famous in Boston, and it is really, really good."
> —Maeve, 13, Hingham, MA

- **Pasta at Maggiano's Little Italy** (4 Columbus Ave.; 617-542-3456; maggianos.com).

- **Cupcakes at Sweet Cupcakes,** where you might try flavors you've never seen. Have you ever had a Boston cream pie cupcake? There are locations at 225 Newbury St., Harvard Square, 49 Massachusetts Ave. in Back Bay, and 11 School St. on the Freedom Trail (sweetcupcakes.com).

- **Dim sum,** which are Chinese dumplings, for brunch in Boston's **Chinatown** (most of the restaurants are along Beach and Tyler Streets and Harrison Avenue).

- **Clam chowder** or a **lobster roll** at a seafood restaurant like **Legal Sea Foods.** Legal has a number of locations throughout Boston, but Legal Harborside has catch-and-release fishing for kids on weekends at lunchtime (270 Northern Ave.; 617-477-2900; legalseafoods.com).

- **Burgers at Tasty Burger** (1301 Boylston St. and two other locations; 617-425-4444; tastyburger .com). The beef is all natural; the buns and hot dogs made locally, and all the sauces are fresh. The company has been run by the same family for 100 years.

A VISITING KID SAYS:
"Kids should not leave Boston without trying Italian food from the North End."
—Oona, 14, Portland, ME

TELL THE ADULTS:

Kids don't want to be limited to kids' menus. Nor do you want them eating a steady diet of chicken fingers and fries on vacation. Of course, you want to treat yourselves and sample the food a city is famous for—like Boston seafood. But we all want to eat healthier on vacation too. First Lady Michelle Obama has made combating childhood obesity and eating healthy a top priority with her "Let's Move!" campaign (letsmove.gov). Here's how she suggests you eat healthier on vacation:

- Planning ahead and packing nutritious snacks whenever possible are a good way to avoid resorting to less healthy options.

- Choose restaurants that offer healthier options and call on other businesses to make similar changes.

- Visit a farmers' market with the kids.

- Get the kids thinking about vacation as an adventure for their taste buds as much as a chance to explore new places.

HOW DO YOU EAT A LOBSTER?

Put these steps in order from 1 to 5.

_____ Push the meat with your finger from the tip of the claw out of the larger open end.

_____ Take off the claws and twist off the loose part of the claw.

_____ Dip in butter and enjoy!

_____ Twist and separate the tail section and then push the tail meat out. (You may need help or a knife to open the tail section).

_____ Use a nutcracker to crack the claw.

See page 155 for the answer key.

DID YOU KNOW?

Lobsters don't have bones or a skeleton like people do. They have a hard outer shell to protect them. This is called an "exoskeleton." Their shell is greenish brown when they are alive, but it turns red when cooked.

10

Beyond Boston:
Cape Cod, Salem & Plymouth Rock

Ready to hit the beach?

You have your pick on **Cape Cod** and the islands of Nantucket and Massachusetts offshore. Most families visit in summer, but it's also fun to visit other times of the year, though it will be too cold to swim.

The distance from Boston to Cape Cod is only about 75 miles, but be prepared—it can be a long drive in summer because everyone wants to go there to play on the beach!

Look at a map to see how Cape Cod juts out into the ocean kind of like a big incomplete letter C or an outstretched arm.

A LOCAL KID SAYS:
"Go to the beaches, go go-karting, minigolfing, and to Chatham Center."
—Arianna, 13, Walpole, MA

DID YOU KNOW?

Before the Pilgrims landed in Plymouth, they arrived at Provincetown at the tip of Cape Cod. They sailed on because they couldn't find a good source of fresh water.

It extends 60 miles into the Atlantic and is just 20 miles at its widest point!

The hardest part will be deciding which beach to visit first. There are 115 to choose from.

You'll see fantastic beaches, cranberry bogs, and light-houses at the **Cape Cod National Seashore** (nps.gov/caco), where a lot of families come to play. You can camp in some spots here too.

Many kids like to bike on the **Cape Cod Rail Trail.** It's mostly flat, and there are many places where you can get off the trail and go to the beach.

A LOCAL KID SAYS:
"I love the Cape! I love to go to the beach there, do fun water activities like tubing, and I especially like to eat ice cream there!"
—Marianna, 13, Walpole, MA

What's Cool? A bike ride on the Cape Cod Rail Trail. It runs for 22 miles through many towns.

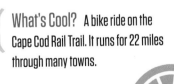

There are 15 towns on Cape Cod chock-full of shops, restaurants, and homemade ice cream stores. Plymouth is where the Pilgrims established the first European settlement in New England and is considered the gateway to the Cape. Many consider Hyannis the Capitol of the Cape because it is the transportation hub for getting to the outer islands of Nantucket and Martha's Vineyard.

Locals divide the towns and beaches of the Cape into:

The Outer Cape—Eastham, Wellfleet, Truro, and Provincetown.

The Upper Cape—Bourne, Sandwich, Falmouth, and Mashpee.

Mid-Cape—Hyannis, Barnstable, Yarmouth, and Dennis.

Lower Cape—Harwich, Brewster, Chatham, and Orleans.

You'll have fun wherever you go. And when you get tired of building sand forts and splashing in the water, you can sail, canoe, kayak, fish, water-ski, or surf. Let's not forget minigolf. There are at least 10 minigolf courses. Local and visiting kids especially like **Pirate's Cove in South Yarmouth** (728 Main St., South Yarmouth; 508-394-6200; piratescove.net).

A VISITING KID SAYS:
"My favorite thing is skimboarding on the sandbars at Coast Guard Beach (on Cape Cod). I love the beautiful sunsets. I've gone biking on the roads, and it's a lot of fun."
—Colleen, 10, Weston, CT

No worries if it rains either. There are lots of museums—kids like the **Heritage Museums & Gardens** with its vintage cars and old carousel in Sandwich (67 Grove St., Sandwich; 508-888-3300; heritagemuseumsandgardens.org).

If it's not a beach day or you're here in the fall, visit a lighthouse, like the Cape Cod Highland Lighthouse in Truro, Cape Cod's oldest. Locals call it **Highland Light** (capecodlight.org). There are still eight working lighthouses on Cape Cod—one of the largest groups of lighthouses anywhere.

Some families take the **ferry to Nantucket or Martha's Vineyard** for the day; others spend their whole vacation there. Some lucky kids get to spend their entire summer on the islands swimming, biking, fishing, and eating home-made fudge. Many families take their dogs and their cars on the ferries. It can be a lot harder to get a reservation for your car than for just you!

Don't forget the sunscreen!

A LOCAL KID SAYS:
"I like to sail and swim and go tubing on Cape Cod and at Martha's Vineyard. I like jumping off of Jaws Bridge. Martha's Vineyard is really pretty."
—Louise, 12, Milton, MA

The First Thanksgiving

Very little is really known about the First Thanksgiving. It was in 1621, and the Pilgrims were glad they'd survived—many of the original settlers didn't—and had gathered the harvest. The Wampanoag Indians, who had helped them, joined in the feast and celebration.

The first national Thanksgiving was proclaimed by the Continental Congress, and by the 1850s, nearly everyone celebrated the holiday. But it wasn't until 1941 that the US Congress permanently established the holiday on the fourth Thursday of November. We eat turkey, cranberries, pumpkin pie,

A VISITING KID SAYS:
"I like going to Plymouth. The water is calmer, shallower, and there's a lot of museums."
—Christopher, 10, Palm Beach Gardens, FL

and sweet potatoes because these are based on New England's fall harvests.

You'll learn more about what life was like for those first settlers and the Wampanoag who were here when they arrived when you visit **Plimoth Plantation** (137 Warren Ave., Plymouth; 508-746-1622; plimoth.org). You can travel back to 1627 where the historic interpreters—including kids—don't get out of character, so you need to learn to "speak Pilgrim."

You can watch—or even help—as they cook, plant, and take care of animals. You can visit the Wampanoag home site too. While you are in Plymouth, you'll also want to step aboard the *Mayflower II,* a replica of the ship that brought the Pilgrims here. It's so small! Imagine what it must have been like on their long voyage—66 days—from England.

Plymouth Rock is right near the *Mayflower II,* and thousands come to see it because they believe it was where the Pilgrims stepped first when they got off the ship. No one really knows for sure.

What do you think?

The Witch City

How could it have happened? Several girls from around Salem, Massachusetts, got sick and accused some people in town of casting spells on them.

What do you think would have happened today? In 1692 more than 150 men and women were charged with practicing witchcraft on the flimsiest evidence, and 20 were put to death.

You can learn more about how such hysteria took over a community if you visit **Salem** (salem.org) just 16 miles from Boston.

There's the **Salem Witch Museum** (Washington Square; 978-744-1692; salemwitchmuseum.com) and a **Salem Witch Trials Memorial** (off Liberty Street).

But there is a lot more to see and do here too. Salem developed into a major fishing and shipbuilding center, and the town grew and prospered. The **Peabody Essex Museum** (East India Square, 161 Essex St., Salem; 978-745-9500; pem.org) celebrates the maritime history here.

There's also literary history in the area. Famous US novelist Nathaniel Hawthorne was born here, and you can visit the **House of Seven Gables** made famous by his novel (115 Derby St., Salem; 978-744-0991; 7gables.org). Can you find the secret staircase?

Talk Like a Surfer

When you surf, you ride on the forward face of a wave toward shore. It's harder than it looks! At least you can talk like a surfer! They have a language of their own.

A **gremmie** is a beginning surfer. He'd be stoked (very happy) to be on these beaches, but might end up taking gas (losing control). Surfers call really great waves all time. Here's some more surfer lingo:

Bail: To step off the board in order to avoid being knocked off.

Shoulder: The unbroken part of the wave.

Gnarly: Large, difficult waves.

Bomb: An exceptionally large wave.

Pop-Up: Going from lying on the board to sanding—in one jump!

Quiver: A surfer's collection of boards.

A LOCAL KID SAYS:
"I like to go to Nantasket Beach and go swimming."
—Alec, 10, Sharon, MA

Beach Smarts

Beaches can be a lot of fun—but they can be dangerous too. Even in shallow water, wave action can cause you to lose your footing. Here's how the experts say you can keep safe:

- Swim only at a lifeguard-protected beach.

- Never swim alone.

- Always go in feetfirst.

- Be mindful of how far from shore you are. You will need the energy to swim back!

A VISITING KID SAYS:
"We went boogie boarding in the ocean for the first time."
—John, 12, Lockport, IL

- Keep a look out for aquatic life and leave it alone.

- Reapply sunscreen every time you get out of the water.

- Keep hydrated by drinking a lot of water.

What's Cool? Going fishing or sailing for the first time.

TELL THE ADULTS:

Beach-going is one of the most fun parts of family vacations, and Massachusetts has some of the most terrific beaches in the country. But swimming in the ocean is different than in a lake or a pool. Rip currents cause deaths at beaches every year—and account for most lifeguard rescues. Here's how the Red Cross says you can keep your family safe:

- Pay especially close attention to children when at the beach. Have young children or inexperienced swimmers wear US Coast Guard–approved life jackets in and around the water.

- Make sure the kids know that if they are caught in a rip current, they must stay calm and not fight the current.

DID YOU KNOW?

Sperm whales were valuable in the 18th and 19th centuries for their "spermaceti oil." This was used for making candles said to burn longer and brighter than any other candle in the world. Nantucket was the center of the whale industry for more than 100 years, until the discovery of petroleum provided a cheaper source of oil.

- If you get caught in a rip current, swim parallel to the shore until out of the current. Only then, turn and swim toward shore.

- If you can't swim to the shore, float or tread water until you are free of the rip current and then head toward shore.

- If you feel you can't make it to the shore, draw attention to yourself by waving and calling for help.

- Stay at least 100 feet away from piers and jetties. Permanent rip currents often exist near these structures.

- If someone is in trouble in the water, get help from a lifeguard. If a lifeguard is not available, have someone call 9-1-1. Throw the victim something that floats—a life jacket, cooler, or inflatable ball perhaps—and yell instructions on how to escape the current.

Draw what you saw!

What a Trip!

I came to Boston with:

_____

_____

_____

The weather was:

_____

_____

_____

We went to:

_____

_____

_____

We ate:

_____

_____

_____

We bought:

_____

_____

_____

I saw these famous Boston sites:

_____

_____

_____

My favorite thing about Boston was:

_____

_____

_____

My best memory of Boston is:

_____

_____

_____

My favorite souvenir is:

_____

_____

_____

_____

_____

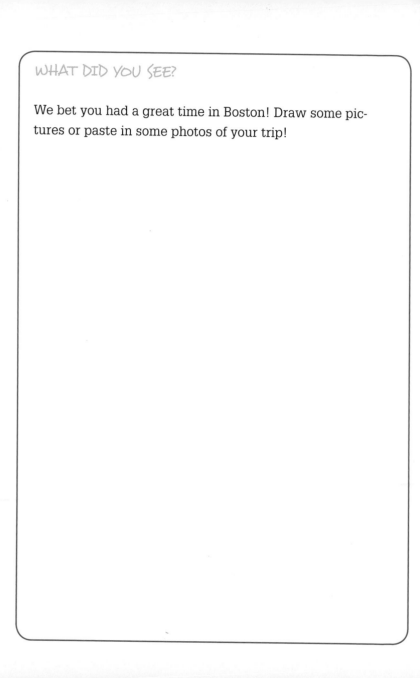

WHAT DID YOU SEE?

We bet you had a great time in Boston! Draw some pictures or paste in some photos of your trip!

Index

Answer Keys

Boston "Firsts" Scramble (p. 13)

1. SCHOOL
2. PUBLIC LIBRARY
3. PUBLIC PARK
4. BOTANICAL GARDEN
5. LIGHTHOUSE
6. MEETING HOUSE

Historic Boston (p. 29)

Boston CoMmon
          (7)
Golden Dome
        (5)
BEacon Hill
 (3)
Park StrEet Church
        (4)
GrAnary Burying GRound
  (9)   (2)
KIng's Chapel
(10)
Boston Latin School
        (11)
Old South Meeting House
(6)

Old STate House

(8)

Faneuil Hall

(1)

Answer:

F R E E D O M T R A I L
(1) (2) (3) (4) (5) (6) (7) (8) (2) (9) (10) (11)

Secret Word Puzzle (p. 40)

Old Ironsides

Word Search: College Central (p. 99)

B	O	S	T	O	N	U	N	I	V	E	R	S	I	T	Y
A	O	A	B	V	A	S	U	V	S	E	T	O	W	D	R
B	M	S	M	R	C	O	E	U	E	G	A	A	N	G	O
E	B	R	T	B	S	I	M	M	O	N	S	L	O	T	T
R	R	E	C	O	F	A	E	B	A	H	T	R	R	N	A
T	A	A	N	L	N	E	R	R	R	T	T	A	T	A	V
U	N	T	Q	L	C	C	S	V	P	Y	S	O	H	B	R
F	D	A	Z	B	O	N	O	M	N	S	E	S	E	T	E
T	E	R	Y	O	C	C	N	L	A	E	G	S	A	P	S
S	I	I	O	R	A	H	L	M	L	T	R	I	S	R	N
Y	S	O	Y	E	L	S	E	L	L	E	W	L	T	I	O
J	U	S	M	S	O	C	D	N	A	L	G	N	E	W	C
E	C	M	I	T	N	R	S	E	W	R	E	E	R	O	E
B	E	R	K	L	E	E	M	O	N	I	C	A	N	Q	N